Circle the stories that are found i

Genesis

Creation of the World	Noah builds the ark
Jesus turns water into wine	Joseph reunites with his brothers
Nehemiah rebuilds the wall	Jesus feeds the five thousand
Peter walks on water	Joseph gets thrown into a pit
David sings for Saul	Solomon builds the temple
Sampson gets a haircut	Job sits with his friends
Joseph interprets dreams	Solomon asks for wisdom
Paul sings in prison	Enoch walks with God
Sodom and Gomorrah are destroyed	Adam and Eve sin
Moses is put into a basket	Jacob gets married...twice
Jonah pouts under a tree	Daniel is thrown into the lion's den
Jacob dies	Abraham is going to sacrifice his son
Cain kills Abel	Jonathon shoots an arrow
Ruth meets Boaz	Jacob steals Esau's birthright
Issac gets married	Moses leads the people out of Egypt
The flood wipes out everything (except the ark)	Gideon blows his trumpet

Draw a picture that describes this part of the Bible story:

Gideon and his army blowing the trumpets and breaking the jars to let their light shine and attacking the sleeping enemy. (Judges 7:19-23)

Date:

My favorite song today was:

How many people are at church today

Write 6 words you hear the pastor say.

The Bible passage today is:

Who can I pray for during the invitation today?

I need to ask my parents to explain....

Today's sermon teaches me about:

Find the words hidden below.

J	X	O	P	R	I	G	H	T	E	O	U	S	Q	R	T	B	V	Z	M
O	O	U	T	V	H	M	N	E	R	V	C	U	K	L	M	P	E	K	W
Y	Q	W	E	R	T	Y	U	W	O	R	L	D	I	O	P	A	S	I	S
S	D	F	G	H	J	K	L	Z	X	C	V	B	N	G	M	P	L	N	G
O	T	K	E	A	R	T	H	M	I	J	N	U	H	L	B	Y	S	G	N
G	R	V	T	F	C	R	D	X	E	S	S	Z	W	O	A	Q	I	M	I
L	A	N	V	C	X	Z	L	K	J	A	H	G	F	R	D	S	N	A	S
O	E	P	O	I	U	Y	T	R	E	V	W	Q	Z	Y	A	Q	G	X	S
V	H	E	A	V	E	N	S	W	C	I	D	E	V	F	R	B	G	T	E
E	N	H	Y	M	J	U	K	I	L	O	O	P	L	K	A	E	D	T	L
U	H	G	T	P	L	K	U	Q	S	R	D	R	T	H	J	I	K	B	B

Joy	Righteous	World
Love	Heart	Earth
Heaven	Savior	Sing
King	Blessings	Glory

Draw a picture of the pastor and get his autograph.

Date:

My favorite song today was:

How many people are wearing black?

Order the Old Testament books by writing the number on top of the word.

Joshua	1 Kings	Ruth
1 Chronicles	Exodus	1 Samuel
1 Genesis	Leviticus	Ezra
Judges	Job	2 Chronicles
2 Samuel	Deuteronomy	Esther
2 Kings	Nehemiah	Numbers

The Bible passage today is:

Who can I pray for during the invitation today?

? I need to ask my parents to explain....

Today's sermon teaches me about:

Find the words hidden below.

M	Z	X	K	I	N	G	V	B	N	J	M	A	S	D	F	G	H	J	M
A	K	L	Q	W	E	R	T	Y	U	I	O	O	P	Z	A	Q	X	S	O
N	W	E	A	N	G	E	L	S	D	C	R	Y	F	V	T	G	B	U	U
G	J	M	I	K	L	O	P	I	H	O	P	E	O	A	N	J	T	I	N
E	A	S	L	D	F	G	H	N	J	K	L	P	O	U	U	U	I	Y	T
R	E	R	O	T	Y	U	I	G	O	P	A	S	D	C	S	B	J	L	A
U	J	M	V	E	D	C	A	I	E	B	A	B	Y	N	M	I	E	C	I
B	A	N	E	S	O	O	N	N	I	K	O	L	P	M	I	L	D	E	N
Q	W	E	R	T	Y	U	I	G	L	O	R	Y	O	P	L	E	K	J	S
H	G	F	D	S	A	Z	X	C	V	B	P	R	A	I	S	E	B	N	M
S	H	E	P	H	E	R	D	S	Q	A	Z	X	S	W	E	D	C	U	I

Angels	Singing	Mountains
Joyous	Shepherds	Manger
Praise	Love	Jubilee
Baby	King	Glory

Draw a picture of the choir singing and get the Minister of Music's autograph.

My favorite song today was:

How many sneezes did I hear?

Date:

Order the New Testament books by writing the number on top of the word.

Mark	2 Corinthians	Galatians
1 Thessalonians	Titus	John
Romans	Philippians	2 Timothy
Luke	Philemon	1 Corinthians
1 Timothy	Ephesians	2 Thessalonians
Acts	Colossians	Ma1hew

The Bible passage today is:

Who can I pray for during the invitation today?

? I need to ask my parents to explain....

Today's sermon teaches me about:

Find the words hidden below.

A	S	K	I	N	G	E	D	G	H	Y	U	O	R	I	E	N	T	N	K
A	S	D	I	T	Y	H	S	T	A	R	R	Y	E	Y	E	G	Q	Z	F
M	N	O	I	N	U	T	R	E	D	F	G	H	K	L	O	L	Q	A	O
I	G	O	I	N	G	Q	A	Z	W	S	X	E	D	L	C	O	R	F	L
V	I	T	G	B	Y	S	H	N	U	J	M	I	D	K	O	R	L	P	L
Y	F	Q	W	E	R	T	Y	M	Y	R	R	H	U	I	O	I	P	A	O
O	T	U	N	D	O	A	S	D	F	G	G	H	J	K	L	O	P	O	W
N	S	E	F	R	A	N	K	I	N	C	E	N	S	E	J	U	K	O	I
D	I	E	U	Y	T	R	E	W	Q	A	S	E	F	T	Y	S	J	I	N
E	O	N	W	O	R	S	H	I	P	P	Z	S	D	C	G	H	M	K	G
R	L	S	A	S	E	F	G	Y	J	K	F	A	R	R	E	A	C	H	S

Kings	Gifts	Star
Gold	Frankincense	Myrrh
Glorious	Worship	Orient
Following	Yonder	Far

Draw a picture of the person that . leading the singing.

Date:

My favorite song today was:

How many people are wearing red today?

My pastor's name is:

My minister of music's name is:

My Sunday School teacher's name is:

The Bible passage today is:

Who can I pray for during the invitation today?

? I need to ask my parents to explain....

Today's sermon teaches me about:

Find the words hidden below.

S	T	O	R	Y	A	S	R	T	I	M	E	S	D	S	L	E	G	N	A
I	O	N	A	W	O	R	D	A	D	I	P	R	E	C	I	O	U	S	N
M	A	S	A	D	F	T	H	U	O	I	E	M	B	U	R	P	D	C	I
C	R	I	A	N	T	A	E	I	R	U	T	O	S	W	S	E	E	R	T
R	O	I	C	U	G	C	A	S	T	T	I	S	W	I	B	N	A	N	S
O	C	R	R	R	A	O	R	P	R	E	R	A	B	P	N	W	W	W	E
S	E	E	O	R	D	S	D	R	P	A	W	S	T	A	R	Y	O	I	T
S	O	N	S	P	A	A	P	E	A	C	E	T	S	W	E	E	R	T	E
A	S	E	T	F	G	Y	U	I	I	N	M	I	I	O	P	W	M	E	E
E	E	D	R	H	E	A	R	E	D	T	C	S	A	A	O	P	I	L	W
P	A	D	A	S	E	R	T	V	G	R	E	M	M	U	P	I	O	S	S

Story	Write	Heart
Word	Precious	Sweetest
Heard	Angels	Sin
Peace	Cross	Paid

Draw a picture of your Sunday School teacher and get their autograph.

Date:

My favorite song today was:

What colors are in the stained glass windows?

Write 6 words you heard the pastor say.

The Bible passage today is:

Who can I pray for during the invitation today?

I need to ask my parents to explain....

Today's sermon teaches me about:

Find the words hidden below.

M	Z	X	K	I	S	N	O	W	I	M	E	S	M	A	S	D	F	G	H
B	U	R	D	E	N	X	S	E	F	I	P	R	O	O	P	Z	A	Q	X
N	W	E	A	N	G	T	H	U	O	I	E	M	R	Y	F	O	T	G	B
P	J	M	I	K	L	W	O	N	D	E	R	S	P	E	O	A	W	J	L
R	A	S	L	D	F	C	A	S	T	T	I	S	L	P	O	U	U	E	O
E	E	R	O	T	W	H	I	T	E	R	R	A	A	S	D	C	S	B	O
C	J	M	C	L	E	A	N	S	I	N	G	A	A	B	Y	N	M	I	D
I	A	N	E	S	O	W	A	S	H	E	S	D	O	L	P	M	I	L	D
O	W	N	R	T	Y	Y	U	I	I	N	M	I	R	Y	O	P	L	E	K
U	I	F	D	L	A	M	B	E	D	T	C	S	P	R	A	I	S	E	B
S	H	E	P	H	E	R	T	V	G	S	E	Y	W	O	R	K	I	N	G

Burden	Power	Sin
Whiter	Snow	Lamb
Precious	Cleansing	Wonder
Working	Blood	Washes

Draw a picture of the Children's Minister and get their autograph.

My favorite song today was:

How many people did I greet today?

Date:

Circle the items you see in your worship area.

Flowers	Microphones	Hymnals
Candles	Speakers	Offering Plates
Water	Cables	Windows
Rafters	Projector Screen	Cushions
Chandeliers	Pencils	Chairs
Piano	Cross	Doors

The Bible passage today is:

Who can I pray for during the invitation today?

? I need to ask my parents to explain....

Today's sermon teaches me about:

Find the words hidden below.

P	C	R	R	R	A	O	R	P	R	E	R	A	B	P	N	W	W	H	E
R	P	R	A	Y	E	R	S	E	E	M	E	S	D	S	L	E	G	E	A
A	A	N	O	W	O	R	D	A	D	I	P	R	E	C	I	O	U	A	N
I	R	S	A	W	F	T	H	U	E	I	E	M	B	U	R	P	D	V	I
S	A	I	A	N	N	A	E	I	E	U	T	O	S	W	S	E	E	E	T
E	D	K	I	N	G	E	D	G	M	Y	U	O	R	I	E	N	T	N	K
C	I	S	U	M	Y	H	S	T	E	R	R	Y	E	Y	E	G	Q	L	F
M	S	O	L	N	U	T	R	E	R	F	G	H	K	L	O	L	Q	Y	O
G	E	A	R	I	F	Y	E	D	E	S	C	E	P	T	E	R	S	N	O
V	M	T	T	H	R	O	N	E	U	J	M	I	D	K	O	R	L	P	L
B	A	D	A	S	E	R	T	V	G	R	E	M	R	E	W	O	P	S	E

Crown	Lamb	Throne
Heavenly	Music	Praise
Glorified	Redeemer	Scepter
Power	Prayer	Paradise

Draw a picture of the person that is sitting in front of you.

Date:

My favorite song today was:

How many people do I count in the pew.

What are the 5 books of poetry in the Bible?

The Bible passage today is:

What are the 4 gospel books in the Bible?

Who can I pray for during the invitation today?

?

I need to ask my parents to explain....

Today's sermon teaches me about:

Find the words hidden below.

G	A	R	D	E	N	K	A	S	V	K	R	A	B	P	N	W	W	H	B
A	E	B	H	U	L	L	D	I	O	L	E	S	D	S	L	E	G	E	I
M	D	G	A	A	O	A	C	U	I	O	P	R	E	C	I	O	U	A	R
E	S	T	T	H	N	W	U	H	C	N	E	M	B	U	R	P	D	V	D
S	A	I	A	N	N	A	E	I	E	U	T	O	S	W	S	E	E	E	T
W	D	K	I	N	G	E	D	S	I	N	G	I	N	G	I	N	G	N	K
E	I	S	U	M	Y	H	S	O	A	S	T	G	B	U	I	K	M	L	F
E	S	O	L	N	U	T	R	U	A	L	O	N	E	A	S	D	R	Y	O
T	E	A	R	I	F	Y	E	N	A	N	D	Y	D	O	L	E	M	N	O
V	M	T	T	H	R	O	N	D	U	J	M	I	D	K	O	R	L	P	L
T	E	N	D	E	R	A	H	U	S	H	E	M	R	E	W	O	P	S	E

Garden	Walk	Talk
Singing	Melody	Sound
Voice	Sweet	Tender
Alone	Bird	Hush

Draw a picture of the person who brought you to church.

Date:

My favorite song today was:

Who do I see that I know?

Circle the Old Testament books.

Jonah	Exodus	Numbers
Zechariah	Mark	Acts
Titus	Haggai	James
Jude	Matthew	1 Chronicles
Ezra	Romans	2 Corinthians
Philemon	Joel	Hebrews

The Bible passage today is:

Who can I pray for during the invitation today?

? I need to ask my parents to explain....

Today's sermon teaches me about:

Find the words hidden below.

C	H	A	N	G	E	D	A	N	D	B	E	H	O	L	D	E	N	I	P
A	S	P	O	A	N	G	I	L	S	K	N	G	E	L	F	O	L	R	D
Y	K	I	M	E	N	T	S	A	V	I	T	C	H	E	N	G	A	D	S
B	E	H	O	L	T	G	R	A	C	E	R	T	H	U	N	I	E	R	S
S	H	O	M	Z	A	Q	E	W	S	X	A	E	D	C	S	T	G	B	A
K	Y	H	E	N	U	J	M	L	I	K	N	O	L	E	H	P	L	O	V
Y	K	M	N	I	J	N	U	H	B	Y	C	G	V	T	O	F	C	R	I
D	X	E	T	H	U	N	D	E	R	S	E	Z	W	A	U	Q	A	S	O
S	E	D	R	F	T	G	Y	H	U	J	I	K	O	P	T	L	I	J	R
S	L	U	M	B	E	R	I	N	G	Y	G	T	F	R	D	E	D	E	S
W	A	X	D	C	F	V	G	B	H	U	N	F	O	L	D	N	J	M	L

Thunder	Praise	Angel
Shout	Sky	Unfold
Behold	Savior	Moment
Slumbering	Entrance	Changed

Draw a picture of the person that is in your favorite bible story.

Draw a picture of the stained glass window.

Match the character to the Bible story.

Joshua	Released a dove.
Joseph	Staff turned into a snake.
Noah	Stayed with her mother-in-law.
David	Spied into the Promise Land.
Moses	Female judge.
Aaron	Lead Army into Promised Land.
Jonathan	Shot an arrow.
Ruth	Slew a giant.
Caleb	Stole his brother's birthright
Deborah	Caught a lot of fish.
Simon Peter	Struck a rock to get water.
Jacob	Jacob's wife.
Leah	Interpreted the cupbearer's dream.

Draw a map from your house to the church.

My favorite song today was:

What are the colors of the flowers?

Date:

Circle the words you heard the pastor say.

Cross	God	Christmas
Faith	Trust	Mercy
Grace	Love	Follow
Encouragement	Birth	Lie
Sin	Fellowship	Truth
Danger	Sunday	Family

The Bible passage today is:

Who can I pray for during the invitation today?

I need to ask my parents to explain....

Today's sermon teaches me about:

Match the character to the Bible story.

Joseph	Man of wisdom.
Saul	First king of Israel.
Silas	Ate locust.
Paul	Moses' sister.
Mary	Would not let the Israelites leave Egypt.
Solomon	Became Queen and helped save her people.
John the Baptist	Joseph's brother.
Pharaoh	Prophet of God.
Abednego	Interpreted the baker's dream.
Miriam	Jesus' mother.
Esther	Shipwrecked.
Benjamin	Walked in the fiery furnace.
Ezekial	Sang in jail.

Draw a picture of your church.

Date:

My favorite song today was:

What color is the preachers shirt?

Write 6 words you hear the pastor say.

The Bible passage today is:

Who can I pray for during the invitation today?

I need to ask my parents to explain....

Today's sermon teaches me about:

Anagrams

How many words can you make from the following:

THUNDER, PRAISE, WORSHIP

MANGER, SHEPHERD, ANGELS

MOUNTAINS, EVERYWHERE, BORN

Draw your interpretation of this Bible verse.

God is our refuge and strength, a very present help in trouble.

Psalm 46:1

Date:

My favorite song today was:

How many people are wearing black?

Order the Old Testament books by writing the number on top of the word.

1 Job	Ezekiel	Isaiah
Joel	Psalm	Jonah
Lamentations	Hosea	Daniel
Song of Solomon	Habakkuk	Obadiah
Micah	Proverbs	Nahum
Ecclesiastes	Amos	Jeremiah

The Bible passage today is:

Who can I pray for during the invitation today?

? I need to ask my parents to explain....

Today's sermon teaches me about:

Anagrams

How many words can you make from the following:

GARDEN, ALONE, MELODY

FALLING, EAR, SINGING

HUSH, WALK, BIRD

Draw your interpretation of this Bible verse.

Evening and morning and at noon, I will complain and murmur, and He will hear my voice.

Psalm 55:17

Date:

My favorite song today was:

How many sneezes did I hear?

Order the New Testament books by writing the number on top of the word.

1 John	2 Peter	3 John
Colossians	2 Thessalonians	Philemon
2 John	Titus	2 Timothy
1 Timothy	Jude	Ephesians
Hebrews	James	1 Thessalonians
1 Peter	Philippians	Revelation

The Bible passage today is:

Who can I pray for during the invitation today?

? I need to ask my parents to explain....

Today's sermon teaches me about:

Anagrams

How many words can you make from the following:

CLOSER, WALK, THEE

DAILY, WALKING, CLOSE

WORLD, FALTER, CARES

Draw your interpretation of this Bible verse.

When I am afraid, I will put my trust in You.

Psalm 56:3

Date:

My favorite song today was:

How many people are wearing yellow today?

Circle the words you heard the pastor say.

Jesus	Need	Christ
Help	Desperate	Fear
Bible	Follow	Priority
Satan	Love	God
Care	Fellowship	Death
Cross	Faith	Encouragement

The Bible passage today is:

Who can I pray for during the invitation today?

?

I need to ask my parents to explain....

Today's sermon teaches me about:

Anagrams

How many words can you make from the following:

FRUIT, GENTLENESS, PEACE

JOY, PATIENCE, KINDNESS

FAITHFULNESS, LOVE, GOODNESS

Draw your interpretation of this Bible verse.

Jesus said unto him, I am the way, and the truth, and the life; no one comes to the Father but through me.

John 14:6

Date:

My favorite song today was:

How many people did I greet today?

How many men were in the balcony?

How many women were in the balcony?

How many people wait on the table?

The Bible passage today is:

Who can I pray for during the invitation today?

I need to ask my parents to explain....

Today's sermon teaches me about:

Anagrams

How many words can you make from the following:

LOVE, PATIENT, KIND

JEALOUS, BRAG, ARROGANT

BELIEVES, HOPES, ENDURES

Draw your interpretation of this Bible verse.

Whether, then, you eat or drink or whatever you do, do all to the glory of God.

1 Corinthians 10:31

Date:

My favorite song today was:

How many people did I greet today?

Order the New Testament books by writing the number on top of the word.

1 John	1 Peter	Colossians
1 Thessalonians	Philippians	Romans
Galatians	Titus	1 Timothy
Philemon	Acts	2 Corinthians
1 Corinthians	2 Thessalonians	James
2 Timothy	Hebrews	Ephesians

The Bible passage today is:

Who can I pray for during the invitation today?

? I need to ask my parents to explain....

Today's sermon teaches me about:

Anagrams

How many words can you make from the following:

BLESSED, POOR, SPIRIT

GENTLE, MERCIFUL, PURE

PEACEMAKERS, RIGHTEOUSNESS,REJOICE

Draw your interpretation of this Bible verse.

This you know, my beloved brethren. But everyone must be quick to hear, slow to speak, and slow to anger.

James 1:19

Date:

My favorite song today was:

How many people are in the building

Order the Old Testament books by writing the number on top of the word.

Isaiah	Micah	Ezekiel
Amos	Hosea	Zephaniah
Daniel	Jeremiah	Nahum
1 Song of Solomon	Haggai	Joel
Habakkuk	Jonah	Zechariah
Lamentations	Obadiah	Malachi

The Bible passage today is:

Who can I pray for during the invitation today?

? I need to ask my parents to explain....

Today's sermon teaches me about:

Anagrams

How many words can you make from the following:

FASHIONED, UNDERSTAINDING, HANDS

GLAD, WORD, JUDGMENTS

LOVINGKINDNESS, COMFORT, SERVANT

Draw your interpretation of this Bible verse.

(Jesus said) but you will receive power when the Holy Spirit has come upon you; and you shall be My witnesses both in Jerusalem, and in all Judea and Samaria, and even to the remotest part of the earth.

Acts 1:8

Date:

My favorite song today was:

Who do I see that I know?

Write 6 words you hear the pastor say and count how many times he says each word.

The Bible passage today is:

Who can I pray for during the invitation today?

I need to ask my parents to explain....

Today's sermon teaches me about:

Anagrams

How many words can you make from the following:

SHEPHERD, GREEN, PASTURES

QUIET, WATERS, RESTORES

STAFF, COMFORT, OVERFLOWS

Draw your interpretation of this Bible verse.

Bear one another's burdens, and thereby fulfill the law of Christ.

Galatians 6:2

Date:

My favorite song today was:

How many people did I greet today?

Circle the words you heard the pastor say.

Love	God	Christ
Acts	Jacob	Mercy
Death	Patience	Bible
Paul	Grace	Forgiveness
Pray	Life	Amen
Cross	Faith	Encouragement

The Bible passage today is:

Who can I pray for during the invitation today?

? I need to ask my parents to explain....

Today's sermon teaches me about:

Anagrams

How many words can you make from the following:

BOAST, CHARIOTS, HORSES

NAME, MEDITATION, ROCK

RESTORING, SALVATION, LIVES

Draw your interpretation of this Bible verse.

So that at the name of Jesus, every knee will bow of those who are in heaven and on earth and under the earth.

Philippians 2:10

Date:

My favorite song today was:

How many people do I count in the pew with me?

Write 6 words you hear the pastor say and write words that are similar.

The Bible passage today is:

Who can I pray for during the invitation today?

I need to ask my parents to explain….

Today's sermon teaches me about:

Anagrams

How many words can you make from the following:

BLESSED, DELIGHT, MEDITATES

TREE, FIRMLY, STREAMS

SEASON, FRUIT, LEAF

Draw your interpretation of this Bible verse.

Submit therefore to God. Resist the devil and he will flee from you, draw near to God and He will draw near to you.

James 4:7-8

Date:

My favorite song today was:

Who do I see that I know?

Circle the Old Testament characters

Ruth	John	Mark
Jude	Job	Ezra
Hoea	Joel	David
James	Esther	Micah
Jonah	Paul	Elijiah
Silas	Jeremiah	Matthew

The Bible passage today is:

Who can I pray for during the invitation today?

? I need to ask my parents to explain....

Today's sermon teaches me about:

BOGGLE

How many words do you see below?

P	A	S	P	I
F	O	T	E	N
T	U	H	T	O
S	R	A	N	L

Draw your interpretation of this Bible verse.

Yet those who wait for the Lord will gain new strength, they will mount up with wings like eagles, they will run and not get tired, they will walk and not become weary.

Isaiah 40:31

Date:

My favorite song today was:

How many people are wearing green?

Circle the New Testament characters.

Mark	Jude	Jonathon
Enoch	Judas	Galatians
Eve	Philemon	Zacheus
Isaiah	Silas	John
Nehemiah	Titus	Timothy
Peter	Ezra	Joseph

The Bible passage today is:

Who can I pray for during the invitation today?

I need to ask my parents to explain....

Today's sermon teaches me about:

BOGGLE

How many words do you see below?

T	R	I	E	S
E	C	O	U	E
N	L	D	L	N
S	K	N	I	T

Draw your interpretation of this Bible verse.

The Lord is my rock and my fortress and my deliverer, my God, my Rock, in whom I take refuge; my shield and the horn of my salvation, my stronghold.

Psalm 18:2

Date:

My favorite song today was:

How many flowers do I see?

What were the announcements that were made today?

The Bible passage today is:

Who can I pray for during the invitation today?

?

I need to ask my parents to explain....

Today's sermon teaches me about:

BOGGLE

How many words do you see below?

T	U	D	N	E
C	R	O	S	E
I	E	T	E	K
P	A	S	L	A

Draw your interpretation of this Bible verse.

Your word I have treasured in my heart that I may not sin against You.

Psalm 119:11

My favorite song today was:

How many times did we pray today?

Date:

Write 6 words you hear the pastor say.

The Bible passage today is:

Who can I pray for during the invitation today?

? I need to ask my parents to explain....

Today's sermon teaches me about:

BOGGLE

How many words do you see below?

P	L	A	I	L
M	A	N	D	O
A	T	E	E	O
R	E	N	E	S

Draw your interpretation of this Bible verse.

I will lift up my eyes to the mountains; from where shall my help come? My help comes from the Lord, who made heaven and earth.

Psalm 121:1-2

Date:

My favorite song today was:

How many people are wearing black?

Order the Old Testament books by writing the number on top of the word.

Psalm	Ezekiel	Ecclesiastes 1
Hosea	Isaiah	Lamentations
Daniel	Proverbs	Ezra
Song of Solomon	Job	Joel
Jonah	Jeremiah	Esther
Amos	Nehemiah	Obadiah

The Bible passage today is:

Who can I pray for during the invitation today?

? I need to ask my parents to explain....

Today's sermon teaches me about:

BOGGLE

How many words do you see below?

S	I	S	E	E
T	R	O	W	D
O	E	N	A	Y
R	N	E	K	A

Draw your interpretation of this Bible verse.

Set a guard, O Lord, over my mouth; keep watch over the door of my lips.

Psalm 141:3

Date:

My favorite song today was:

How many sneezes did I hear?

Order the New Testament books by writing the number on top of the word.

Mark	2 Corinthians	Galatians
1 Thessalonians	Titus	John
Romans	Philippians	2 Timothy
Luke	Philemon	1 Corinthians
1 Timothy	Ephesians	2 Thessalonians
Acts	Colossians	1 Matthew

The Bible passage today is:

Who can I pray for during the invitation today?

? I need to ask my parents to explain....

Today's sermon teaches me about:

Circle the stories that are found in the book of

Moses is born	Creation of the plants and animals
12 spies are sent to spy the Promise Land	Moses talks to a burning bush
Plague: Death of the firstborn	Sampson pushes the pillars
Peter walks on water	Parting of the Red Sea
Plague of locusts	The walls of Jericho tumble down
Gideon leads the Army	Jesus heals the blind
Cain kills Abel	David slings the rock
Aaron staff turns into a snake	Daniel is thrown into the lions den
Wise men travel to see baby Jesus	Tabernacle built
Deborah is judge	The world is flooded
Jesus raises Lazarus from the dead	Plague of hail
John is imprisoned	Paul is shipwrecked
Moses kills the Egyptian	Saul throws a javelin at David
Lot's wife turns into a pillar of salt	Followed cloud by day
Plague of gnats	Manna falls from heaven
Ten commandments given	Plague of the boils

Draw your interpretation of this Bible verse.

A gentle answer turns away wrath, but a harsh word stirs up anger.

Proverbs 15:1

My favorite song today was:

How many people are wearing red today?

Date:

Write the first 5 books of the Bible.

The Bible passage today is:

Who can I pray for during the invitation today?

I need to ask my parents to explain....

Today's sermon teaches me about:

Unscramble the Bible verse below.

things	do	through	can	me
Him	who	I	strengthens	all

Philippians 4:13

Draw your interpretation of this Bible verse.

Have I not commanded you? Be strong and courageous! Do not tremble or be dismayed, for the Lord your God is with you wherever you go.

Joshua 1:9

Date:

My favorite song today was:

What colors are in the stained glass windows?

Write the first 5 books of the New Testament.

The Bible passage today is:

Who can I pray for during the invitation today?

? I need to ask my parents to explain….

Today's sermon teaches me about:

Unscramble the Bible verse below.

hearing,	and	faith	by	the
word	comes	hearing	from	So
of	Christ			

Romans 10:17

Draw a picture that describes this part of the Bible story:

What did Egypt look like with all the frog? (Exodus 8:1-15)

Date:

My favorite song today was:

How many people did I greet today?

Circle the items you do not see in your worship area.

Flowers	Microphones	Hymnals
Tires	Speakers	Dinner Plates
Water	Fingernail Polish	Windows
Library Books	Projector Screen	Swings
Chandeliers	Slides	Chairs
Roller Coaster	Cross	Water Fountain

The Bible passage today is:

Who can I pray for during the invitation today?

? I need to ask my parents to explain....

Today's sermon teaches me about:

Unscramble the Bible verse below.

that	I	to	commandment	you,
give	you	new	love	A
one	loved	even	you	another
that	you	another	as	love
one	I	have	also	

John 13:34

Draw a picture that describes this part of the Bible story:

What did Egypt look like with all the flies? (Exodus 8:20-30)

Date:

My favorite song today was:

How many windows are in the worship area?

Write the names of 6 Old Testament characters.

The Bible passage today is:

Who can I pray for during the invitation today?

? I need to ask my parents to explain....

Today's sermon teaches me about:

Unscramble the Bible verse below.

with	in	lean	your	In	your
understanding	all	heart	Lord	Him	not
And	He	do	will	all	make
on	own	ways	paths	straight	and
acknowledge	the	your	Trust	your	

Proverbs 3:5-6

Draw a picture that describes this part of the Bible story:

Draw the Red Sea being parted by Moses. (Exodus 14:16-22)

Date:

My favorite song today was:

How many doors are in the worship area?

Draw a map OR write directions you would use to give a guest directions to the bathroom.

The Bible passage today is:

Who can I pray for during the invitation today?

I need to ask my parents to explain....

Today's sermon teaches me about:

Unscramble the Bible verse below.

confess	to	our	to	righteous
cleanse	is	and	sins	us
unrighteousness	He	we	sins	our
faithful	and	from	forgive	If
all				

1 John 1:9

Draw a picture that describes this part of the Bible story:

Draw the walls of Jericho tumbling down. (Joshua 6:1-27)

My favorite song today was:

How many people are wearing blue?

Date:

What announcements did I hear today?

Were any of the announcements related to children's activities?

The Bible passage today is:

Who can I pray for during the invitation today?

I need to ask my parents to explain....

Today's sermon teaches me about:

Unscramble the Bible verse below.

you	it	have	the	God	faith;
by	gift	a	and	saved	as
yourselves,	grace	is	been	of	not
through	not	that	For	of	result
boast	that	no	of	one	works
may	so				

Ephesians 2:8-9

Draw a picture that describes this part of the Bible story:

Draw the foxes running through the fields. (Judges 15:4-5)

Date:

My favorite song today was:

What are the colors of the flowers?

Circle the words you heard the pastor say.

Cross	God	Christmas
Faith	Trust	Mercy
Grace	Love	Follow
Encouragement	Birth	Lie
Sin	Fellowship	Truth
Danger	Sunday	Family

The Bible passage today is:

Who can I pray for during the invitation today?

? I need to ask my parents to explain....

Today's sermon teaches me about:

Unscramble the Bible verse below.

despise	and	is	instruction	Lord
beginning	fear	of	fools	the
knowledge;	of	wisdom	The	the

Proverbs 1:7

Draw a picture that describes this part of the Bible story:

Draw the Philistine idol falling down before the Ark of the Covenant. (1 Samuel 5:1-5)

Date:

My favorite song today was:

How many books are in the New Testament?

Write the words to my favorite song from today.

The Bible passage today is:

Who can I pray for during the invitation today?

? I need to ask my parents to explain....

Today's sermon teaches me about:

Unscramble the Bible verse below.

For	He	that	only	so
begotten	the	God	His	believes
loved	that	in	world	gave
Him	life	whoever	eternal	shall
have				

John 3:16

Draw a picture that describes this part of the Bible story:

Draw David defeating Goliath. (1 Samuel 17:41-49)

Date:

My favorite song today was:

How many people are wearing black?

Write 6 words you hear the pastor say.

What word of those 6 did he use the most?

The Bible passage today is:

Who can I pray for during the invitation today?

? I need to ask my parents to explain....

Today's sermon teaches me about:

Unscramble the Bible verse below.

people	humble	and	from	My	ways;
wicked	by	and	who	pray	face
called	their	My	seek	My	will
themselves	name	and	and	are	turn
from	then	forgive	I	heaven	hear
and	will	their	sin	and	their
land	heal	will			

2 Chronicles 7:14

Draw a picture that describes this part of the Bible story:

Draw the battle between Elijah and the priests of Baal. (1 Kings 14:1-40)

Date:

My favorite song today was:

How many sneezes did I hear?

Order the New Testament books by writing the number on top of the word.

1 John	2 Peter	3 John
Colossians	2 Thessalonians	Philemon
2 John	Titus	2 Timothy
1 Timothy	Jude	1 Ephesians
Hebrews	James	1 Thessalonians
1 Peter	Philippians	Revelation

The Bible passage today is:

Who can I pray for during the invitation today?

I need to ask my parents to explain....

Today's sermon teaches me about:

Fill in the missing vowels to the Bible verse.

Th_ r_ch _nd th_ p__r h_ve a c_mm_n b_nd, th_ L_rd _s th_ m_k_r _f th_m _ll.

Proverbs 22:2

F_r th_ L_rd kn_ws th_ w_y _f th_ r_ght___s, b_t th_ w_y _f th_ w_ck_d w_ll p_r_sh.

Psalm1:6

Draw a picture that describes this part of the Bible story:

Draw the men in the fiery furnace. (Daniel 3:13-30)

Date:

My favorite song today was:

How many people are wearing yellow today?

Circle the words you heard the pastor say.

Jesus	Need	Christ
Help	Desperate	Fear
Bible	Follow	Priority
Satan	Love	God
Care	Fellowship	Death
Cross	Faith	Encouragement

The Bible passage today is:

Who can I pray for during the invitation today?

? I need to ask my parents to explain....

Today's sermon teaches me about:

Fill in the missing vowels to the Bible verse.

H_s d_m_n__n _s _n _v_rl_st_ng
d_m_n__n wh_ch w_ll n_t p_ss _w_y; _nd
H_s k_ngd_m _s _n_ wh_ch w_ll n_t b_
d_str_y_d.

Daniel 7:14d

H_ h_s t_ld y__, O m_n, wh_t _s g__d; _nd
wh_t d__s th_ Lord r_q__r_ _f y__ b_t t_
d_ j_st_c_, t_ l_ve k_ndn_ss, _nd t_ w_lk
h_mbly w_th y__r God.

Micah 6:8

Draw a picture that describes this part of the Bible story:

Draw Daniel in the lion's den. (Daniel 6:12-22)

Date:

My favorite song today was:

How many people did I greet today?

What is the book of the Bible that comes BEFORE the book the Bible passage is taken from?

What is the book of the Bible that comes AFTER the book the Bible passage is taken from?

The Bible passage today is:

Who can I pray for during the invitation today?

? I need to ask my parents to explain....

Today's sermon teaches me about:

Fill in the missing vowels to the Bible verse.

Th_ Lord _s g__d, a str_ngh_ld _n th_ d_y _f tr__bl_, _nd He kn_ws th_s_ wh_ t_k_ r_f_g_ _n Him.

Nahum 1:7

F_r wh_r_ tw_ _r thr__ h_ve g_th_r_d t_g_th_r _n My n_m_, I _m th_r_ _n th__r m_dst.

Matthew 18:20

Draw a picture that describes this part of the Bible story:

Draw the wise man's house. (Matthew 7:24-27)

Date:

My favorite song today was:

How many people did I greet today?

What is the first book of the Bible?

What is the last book of the Bible?

What is the book of the Bible that is the very middle?

The Bible passage today is:

Who can I pray for during the invitation today?

I need to ask my parents to explain....

Today's sermon teaches me about:

Use the code to figure out the Bible verse.

A	B	C	D	E	F	G	H	I	J	K	L	M
1	2	3	4	5	6	7	8	9	10	11	12	13

N	O	P	Q	R	S	T	U	V	W	X	Y	Z
14	15	16	17	18	19	20	21	22	23	24	25	26

6 15 18   1 12 12   8 1 22 5   19 9 14 14 5 4

1 14 4   6 1 12 12 5 14   19 8 15 18 20   15 6

20 8 5   7 12 15 18 25   15 6   7 15 4

Romans 3:23

Draw a picture that describes this part of the Bible story:

Draw the foolish man's house. (Matthew 7:24-27)

Date:

My favorite song today was:

How many books are in the Old Testament?

What book of the Bible do you think is the longest?

What book of the Bible do you think is the shortest?

What is the first book of the New Testament?

What is the last book of the Old Testament?

The Bible passage today is:

Who can I pray for during the invitation today?

I need to ask my parents to explain....

Today's sermon teaches me about:

Use the code to figure out the Bible verse.

A	B	C	D	E	F	G	H	I	J	K	L	M
1	2	3	4	5	6	7	8	9	10	11	12	13

N	O	P	Q	R	S	T	U	V	W	X	Y	Z
14	15	16	17	18	19	20	21	22	23	24	25	26

---

9 6   16 15 19 19 9 12 5   19 15   6 1 18

---

1 19   9 20   4 5 16 5 14 4 19   15 14

---

25 15 21   2 5   1 20   16 5 1 3 5

---

23 9 20 8   1 12 12   13 5 14

Romans 12:18

Draw a picture that describes this part of the Bible story:

Draw the inside of Noah's ark (full of animals). (Genesis 7:1-5)

Date:

My favorite song today was:

Who do I see that I know?

Write 6 words you hear the pastor say and count how many times he says each word.

The Bible passage today is:

Who can I pray for during the invitation today?

? I need to ask my parents to explain....

Today's sermon teaches me about:

Use the code to figure out the Bible verse.

A	B	C	D	E	F	G	H	I	J	K	L	M
1	2	3	4	5	6	7	8	9	10	11	12	13

N	O	P	Q	R	S	T	U	V	W	X	Y	Z
14	15	16	17	18	19	20	21	22	23	24	25	26

6 15 18   14 15   13 1 14   3 1 14

12 1 25   1   6 15 21 14 4 1 20 9 15 14   15 20 8 5 18

20 8 1 14   20 8 5   15 14 5   23 8 9 3 8

9 19   12 1 9 4   23 8 9 3 8   9 19

10 5 19 21 19   3 8 18 9 19 20.

1 Corinthians 3:11

Draw a picture that describes this part of the Bible story:

Draw Joseph's special coat. (Genesis 37:3)

Date:

My favorite song today was:

How many people did I greet today?

Circle the words you heard the pastor say.

Honor	Care	Disciple
Song	Faith	Armor
Goodness	Grace	David
Trust	Encouragement	Will
Salvation	Sin	Peter
Obey	Love	Surrender

The Bible passage today is:

Who can I pray for during the invitation today?

? I need to ask my parents to explain....

Today's sermon teaches me about:

Use the code to figure out the Bible verse.

A	B	C	D	E	F	G	H	I	J	K	L	M
1	2	3	4	5	6	7	8	9	10	11	12	13

N	O	P	Q	R	S	T	U	V	W	X	Y	Z
14	15	16	17	18	19	20	21	22	23	24	25	26

____

20 8 1 14 11 19   2 5   20 15

____

7 15 4   6 14 18   8 9 19

____

9 14 4 5 19 3 18 9 2 1 2 12 5   7 9 6 20

2 Corinthians 9:15

Draw a picture that describes this part of the Bible story:

Draw Joseph reuniting with his brothers. (Genesis 45:1-9)

My favorite song today was:

How many songs did we sing?

Date:

Write 5 books of the Bible that you think are named after a person.

Write the books of the Bible that have more that one (1st, 2nd).

The Bible passage today is:

Who can I pray for during the invitation today?

I need to ask my parents to explain....

Today's sermon teaches me about:

Use the code to figure out the Bible verse.

A	B	C	D	E	F	G	H	I	J	K	L	M
1	2	3	4	5	6	7	8	9	10	11	12	13

N	O	P	Q	R	S	T	U	V	W	X	Y	Z
14	15	16	17	18	19	20	21	22	23	24	25	26

9 6   23 5   12 9 22 5   2 25

20 8 5   19 16 9 18 9 20,   12 5 20   21 19

1 12 19 15   23 1 12 11   2 25   20 8 5

19 16 9 18 9 20.

Galatians 5:25

Draw a picture that describes this part of the Bible story:

Draw Jacob's dream. (Genesis 28:10-14)

My favorite song today was:

Who do I see that I know?

Date:

Write 6 words you hear the pastor say and write what you think each word means.

The Bible passage today is:

Who can I pray for during the invitation today?

?

I need to ask my parents to explain….

Today's sermon teaches me about:

Use the code to figure out the Bible verse.

A	B	C	D	E	F	G	H	I	J	K	L	M
1	2	3	4	5	6	7	8	9	10	11	12	13

N	O	P	Q	R	S	T	U	V	W	X	Y	Z
14	15	16	17	18	19	20	21	22	23	24	25	26

____

1 12 23 1 25 19   7 9 22 9 14 7   20 8 1 14 11 19   6 15 18

____

1 12 12   20 8 9 14 7 19   9 14   20 8 5

____

14 1 13 5   15 6   15 21 18   12 15 18 4

____

10 5 19 21 19   3 8 18 9 19 20   20 15   7 15 4

____

5 22 5 14   20 8 5   6 1 20 8 5 18

Ephesians 5:20

Draw a picture that describes this part of the Bible story:

Draw Zaccheus meeting Jesus. (Luke 19:1-10)

Date:

My favorite song today was:

How many people did I greet today?

Circle the words you heard the pastor say.

Honor	Care	Disciple
Song	Faith	Armor
Goodness	Grace	David
Trust	Encouragement	Will
Salvation	Sin	Peter
Obey	Love	Surrender

The Bible passage today is:

Who can I pray for during the invitation today?

? I need to ask my parents to explain....

Today's sermon teaches me about:

Use the code to figure out the Bible verse.

A	B	C	D	E	F	G	H	I	J	K	L	M
1	2	3	4	5	6	7	8	9	10	11	12	13

N	O	P	Q	R	S	T	U	V	W	X	Y	Z
14	15	16	17	18	19	20	21	22	23	24	25	26

20 8 5 22 15 9 3 5 15 6

20 8 5 12 15 18 4 9 19

16 15 23 5 18 6 21 12 20 8 5 22 15 9 3 5

15 6 20 8 5 12 15 18 4

9 19 13 1 10 5 19 20 9 3

Psalm 29:4

Draw a picture that describes this part of the Bible story:

Draw Peter walking on the water with Jesus. (Matthew 14:22-23)

Date:

My favorite song today was:

How many books are in the bible?

Write the words to your favorite song from today.

The Bible passage today is:

Who can I pray for during the invitation today?

?

I need to ask my parents to explain....

Today's sermon teaches me about:

Unscramble each word of the Bible verse.

utB	het	valtinosa	fo
teh	therigous	si	mfro
the	doLr	eH	si
rieht	ghtsrtne	ni	miet
fo	boultre		

Psalm 29:4

Draw a picture that describes this part of the Bible story:

Draw Paul and Silas singing in jail. (Acts 16:25-31)

My favorite song today was:

Who do I see that I know?

Date:

Write 6 words you hear the pastor say and write what you think each word means.

The Bible passage today is:

Who can I pray for during the invitation today?

I need to ask my parents to explain....

Today's sermon teaches me about:

Unscramble each word of the Bible verse.

sA	eth	edre	nspat
rof	het	retaw	oksobr
os	ym	ulso	napts
ofr	uYo	O	odG

Psalm 42:1

Draw a picture that describes this part of the Bible story:

Draw Simon Peter catching so many fish the nets broke. (Matthew 5:3-11)

38676919R00090

Made in the USA
Lexington, KY
20 January 2015